Recorder Fun!

Songs from
Frozen, Tangled and Enchanted

CONTENTS

SONGS

ISBN 978-1-4803-9670-8

Walt Disney Music Company
Wonderland Music Company, Inc.

DISTRIBUTED BY

HAL•LEONARD®
CORPORATION

7777 W. BLUEMOUND RD. P.O. BOX 13819 MILWAUKEE, WI 53213

In Australia Contact:
Hal Leonard Australia Pty. Ltd.
4 Lentara Court
Cheltenham, Victoria, 3192 Australia
Email: ausadmin@halleonard.com.au

Visit Hal Leonard Online at
www.halleonard.com

GETTING STARTED

HOLDING THE RECORDER

Here is how to hold the recorder. The mouthpiece rests on your lower lip, just like a drinking straw, with only a little of it actually going inside your mouth. Be sure that all of the finger holes line up on the front of the recorder as shown in the picture.

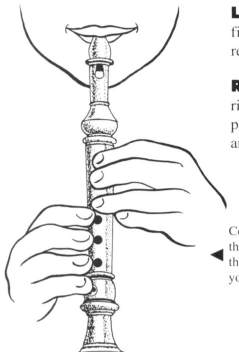

LEFT HAND — The first three fingers of your left hand (the little finger is not used) play the *top* three holes on the front of the recorder. The thumb of your left hand plays the hole on the back.

RIGHT HAND — The *bottom* four holes are played by your right-hand fingers. There is no hole for your right-hand thumb to play so it can help hold the recorder steady while the other fingers are busy playing.

◄ Cover the top three holes with your left-hand fingers and the bottom four holes with your right-hand fingers. The thumb of your left hand covers the hole in the back of your recorder.

MAKING A SOUND

To make a sound on the recorder blow gently into the small opening at the top of the mouthpiece. You can change this sound by covering different holes with your thumb and fingers. For example, when you cover all of the thumb and finger holes you will get a low, quiet sound. When only one or two holes are covered the sound will be higher and much louder.

Here are some tips for getting the best possible sound out of your recorder:

Always blow gently into the mouthpiece — Breathe in and then gently blow into the mouthpiece as if you were sighing or using a straw to blow out a candle. Remember, always blow gently.

Leaks cause squeaks — Play the holes using the pads of your fingers and thumb (not the tips). Press against each hole firmly so that it is completely covered and no air can sneak out. Even a tiny leak of air will change a beautiful tone into a sudden squeak!

Use your tongue to start each tone — Place your tongue against the roof of your mouth just behind your front teeth and start each tone that you play by tonguing the syllable "du" or "too" as you blow gently into the recorder.

PLAYING A TONE

Musical sounds are called *tones*. Every tone has a letter name. *Finger charts* are used to show you exactly which holes should be covered in order to play a particular tone. Each circle on these charts represents one of the holes on your recorder. The thumb hole is represented by the circle to the left of the recorder in the chart.

●   means that you should cover that hole.

○   means that that hole should not be covered but left open.

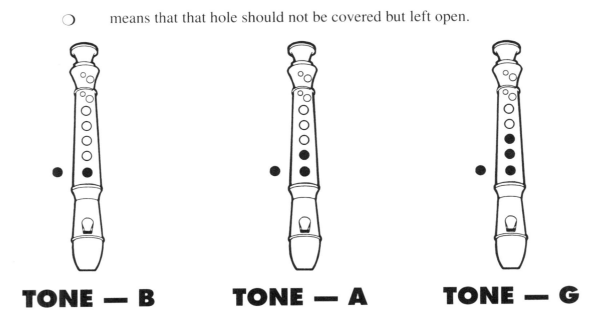

Use these three tones to play "Mary Had A Little Lamb:"

MARY HAD A LITTLE LAMB

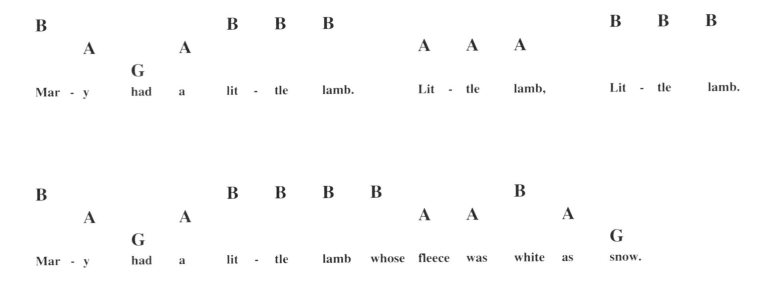

READING MUSIC

Musical notes are an easy way to see everything that you need to know in order to play a song on your recorder:

How high or low — Notes are written on five lines that are called a *staff*. The higher a note is written on the staff the higher it will sound.

How long or short — The color of a note (black or white) tells you if it should be played short or long. The black notes in "Mary Had A Little Lamb" are all one beat long (*quarter notes*). The first three white notes in this song are two beats long (*half notes*) and the last note is four beats long (*whole note*).

How the beats are grouped — The two numbers at the beginning of the song (4/4) are called a *time signature*. This time signature tells you that the *beats* in this song are grouped in fours: **1** 2 3 4 **1** 2 3 4 etc. To help you see this grouping, *bar lines* are drawn across the staff to mark each *measure* of four beats. A *double bar* is used to mark the end of the song.

Now here is how "Mary Had A Little Lamb" looks when it is written in musical notes:

MARY HAD A LITTLE LAMB

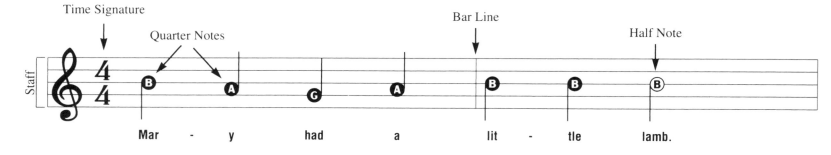

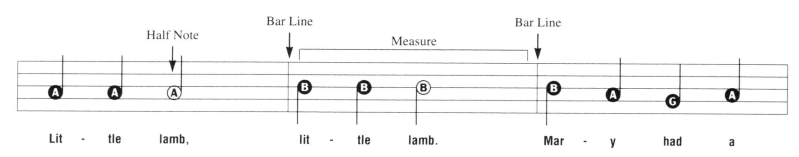

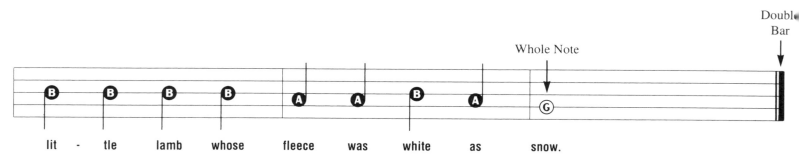

TWO NEW TONES

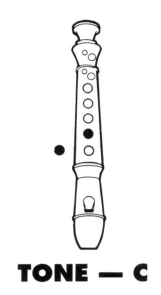

TONE — C

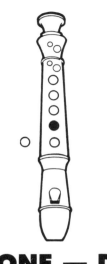

TONE — D

AURA LEE

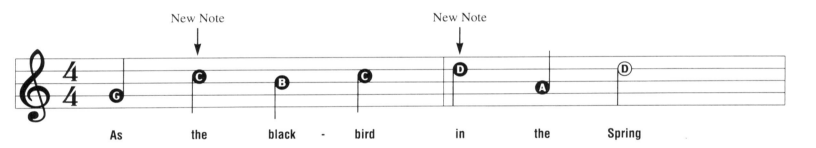

New Note   New Note

As   the   black - bird   in   the   Spring

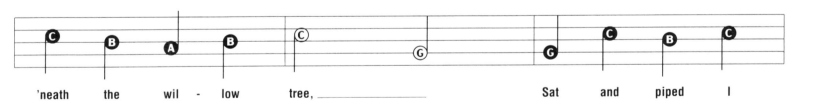

'neath   the   wil - low   tree, _____   Sat   and   piped   I

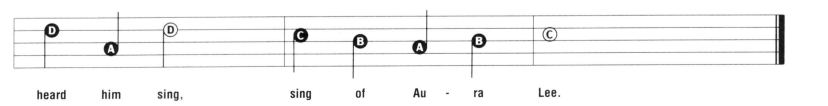

heard   him   sing,   sing   of   Au - ra   Lee.

USING YOUR RIGHT HAND

"Twinkle, Twinkle Little Star" uses the tone E. As you can see from the fingering chart, you will use three fingers of your left hand and two fingers of your right to play this tone. The thumb hole is only half filled in (◑). This means that you should "pinch" the hole with your thumb so that only a small part of the hole is left open. Pinching is done by bending your thumb so that the thumbnail points directly into the recorder leaving the top of the thumb hole open.

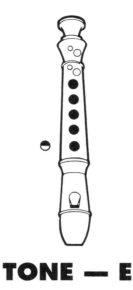

TONE — E

TWINKLE, TWINKLE LITTLE STAR

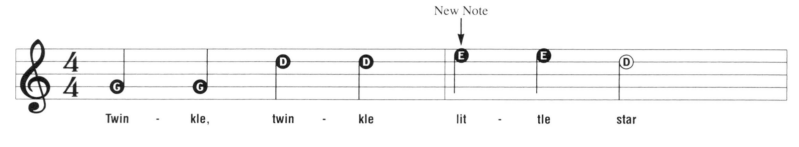

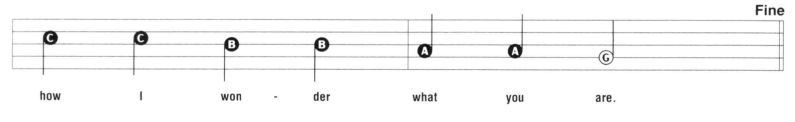

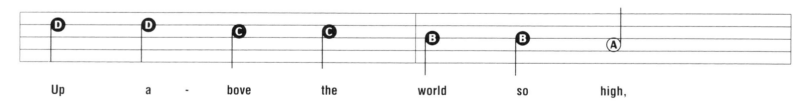

NOTES AND RESTS

In addition to notes that are one, two or four beats long, other values are possible. Also, *rests* are used to indicate when you should *not* play a tone but be silent. The chart on page 7 will help you identify the different notes and rests that are used in this book.

COUNT:

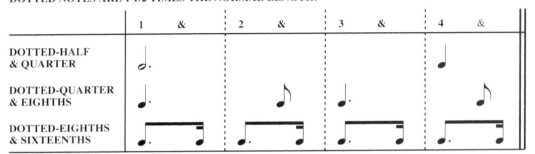

	1	&	2	&	3	&	4	&	NUMBER OF BEATS	REST
WHOLE NOTES									4	
HALF NOTES									2	
QUARTER NOTES									1	
EIGHTH NOTES				(or)					1/2	
& SIXTEENTHS				(or)					1/4	

DOTTED NOTES ARE 1 1/2 TIMES THE NORMAL LENGTH:

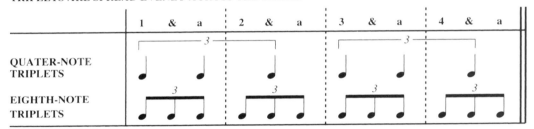

	1	&	2	&	3	&	4	&
DOTTED-HALF & QUARTER								
DOTTED-QUARTER & EIGHTHS								
DOTTED-EIGHTHS & SIXTEENTHS								

TRIPLETS ARE SPREAD EVENLY ACROSS THE BEATS:

	1	&	a	2	&	a	3	&	a	4	&	a
QUATER-NOTE TRIPLETS												
EIGHTH-NOTE TRIPLETS												

THIS OLD MAN

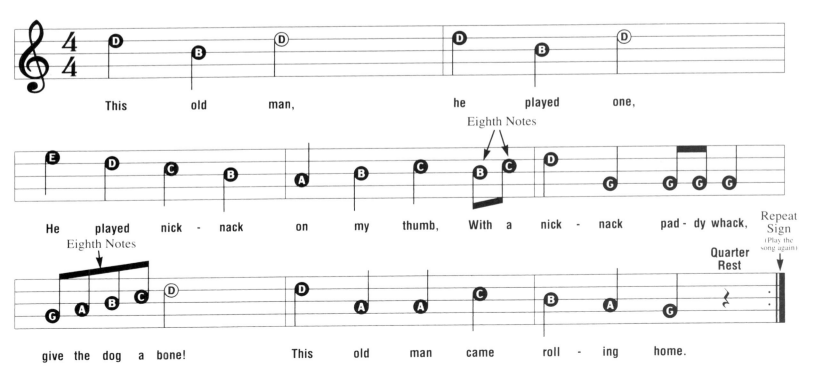

FINGERING CHART

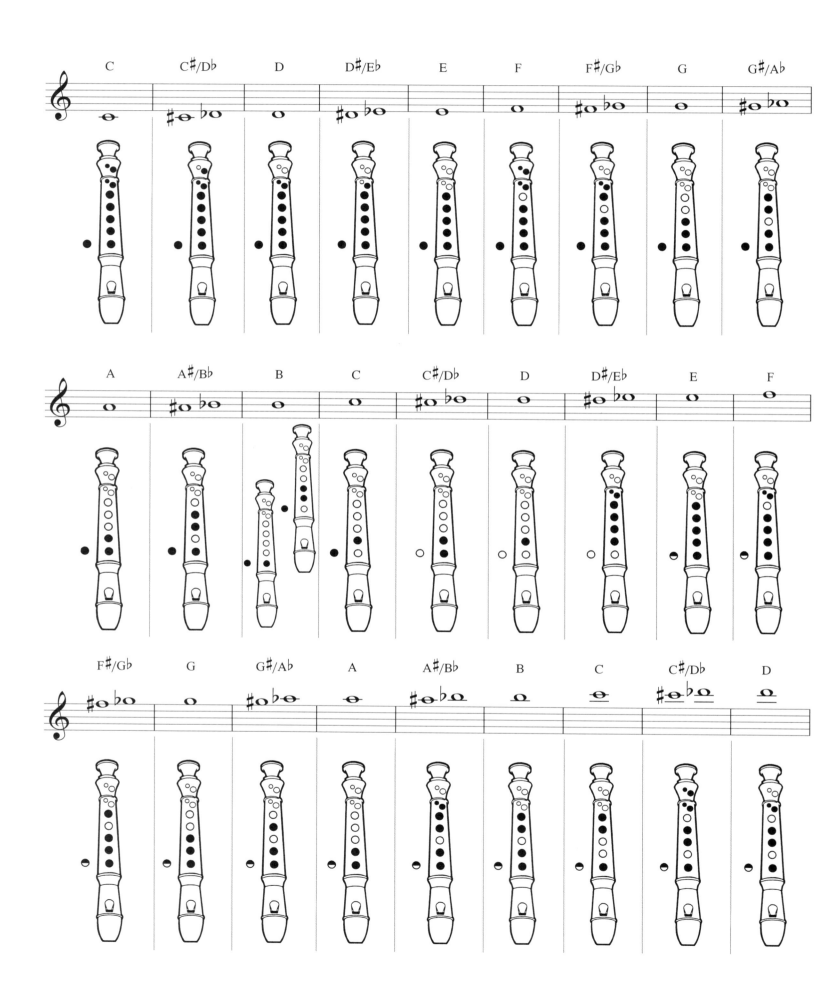

DO YOU WANT TO BUILD A SNOWMAN?

from Disney's Animated Feature FROZEN

Music and Lyrics by Kristen Anderson-Lopez
and Robert Lopez

FOR THE FIRST TIME IN FOREVER

from Disney's Animated Feature FROZEN

Music and Lyrics by Kristen Anderson-Lopez
and Robert Lopez

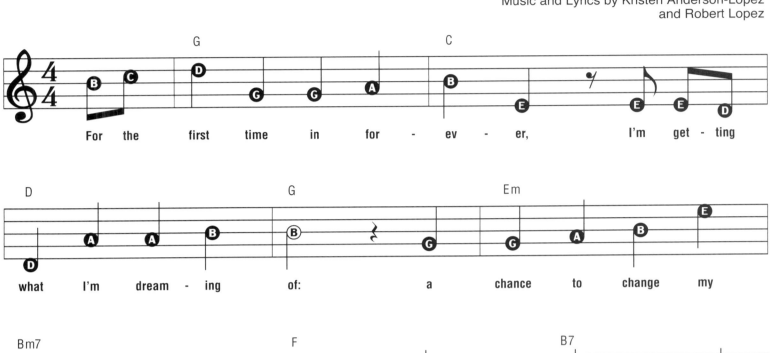

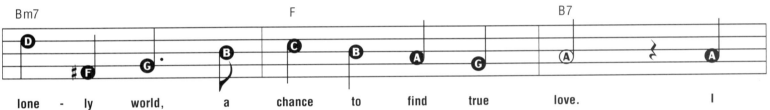

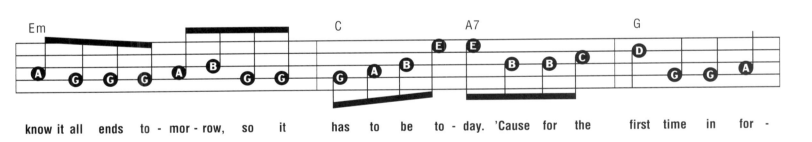

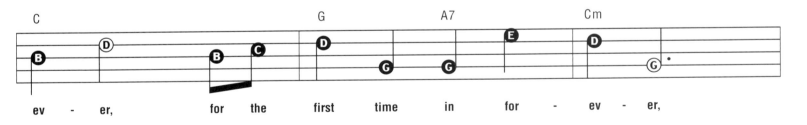

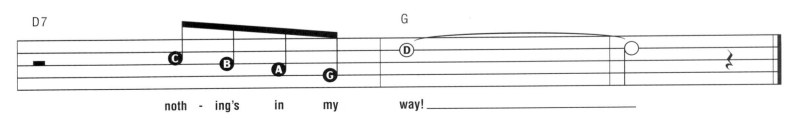

LET IT GO
from Disney's Animated Feature FROZEN

Music and Lyrics by Kristen Anderson-Lopez
and Robert Lopez

I SEE THE LIGHT

from Walt Disney Pictures' TANGLED

Music by Alan Menken
Lyrics by Glenn Slater

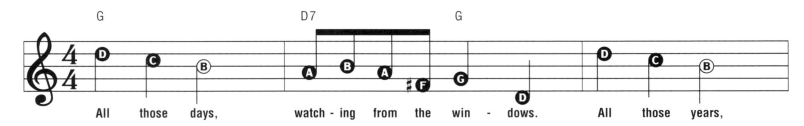

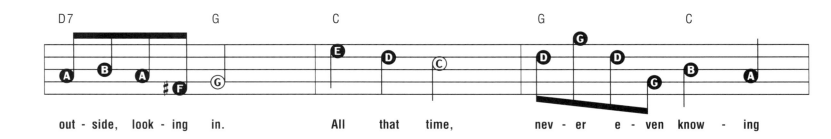

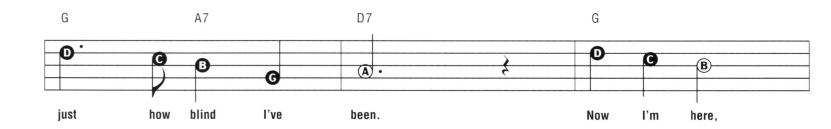

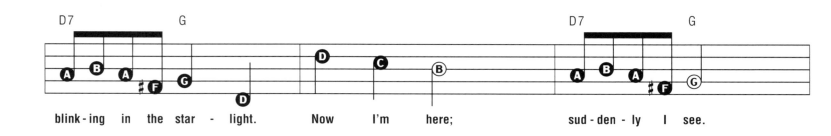

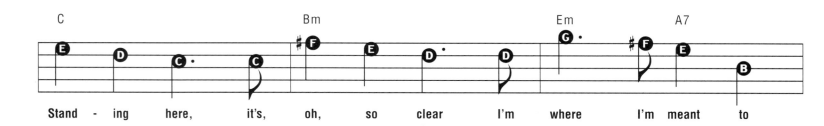

15

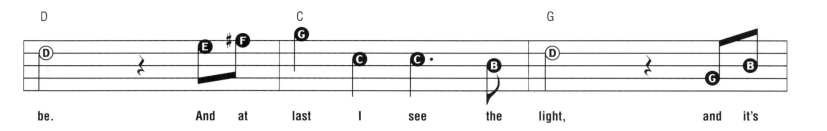

be. And at last I see the light, and it's

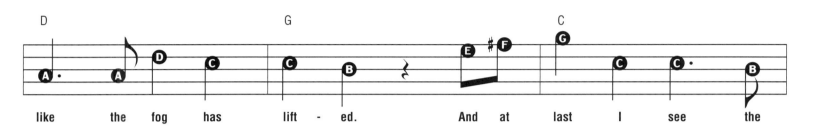

like the fog has lift - ed. And at last I see the

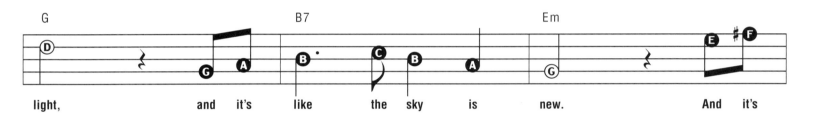

light, and it's like the sky is new. And it's

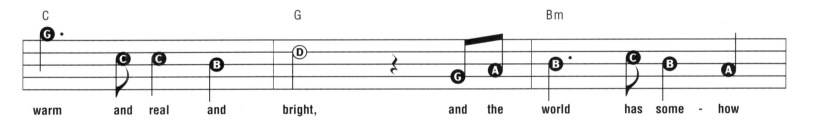

warm and real and bright, and the world has some - how

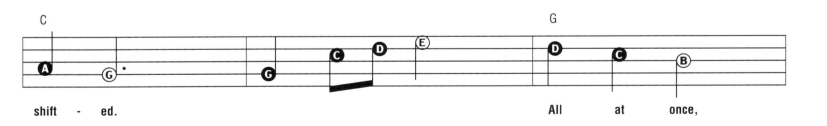

shift - ed. All at once,

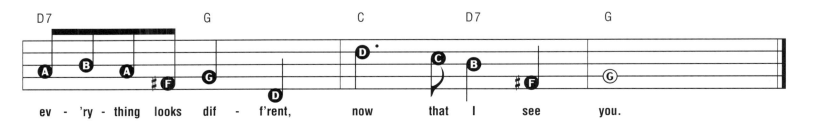

ev - 'ry - thing looks dif - f'rent, now that I see you.

MOTHER KNOWS BEST
from Walt Disney Pictures' TANGLED

Music by Alan Menken
Lyrics by Glenn Slater

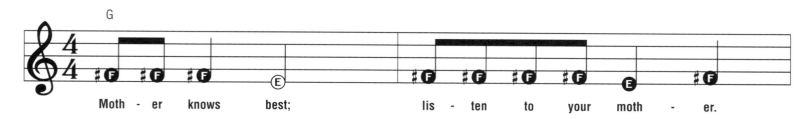

Moth - er knows best; lis - ten to your moth - er.

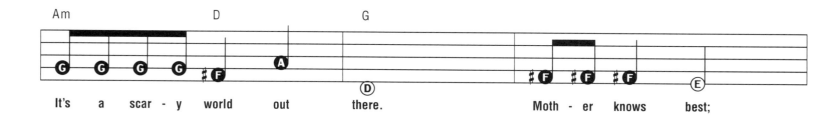

It's a scar - y world out there. Moth - er knows best;

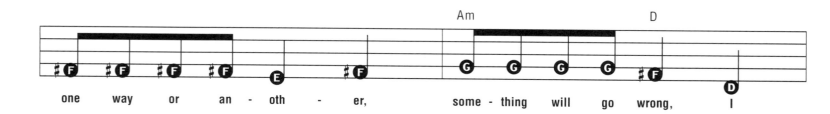

one way or an - oth - er, some - thing will go wrong, I

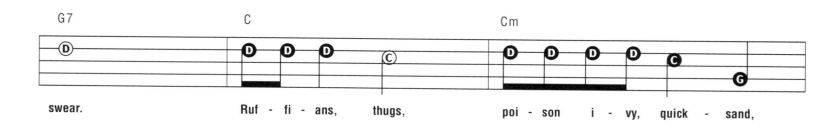

swear. Ruf - fi - ans, thugs, poi - son i - vy, quick - sand,

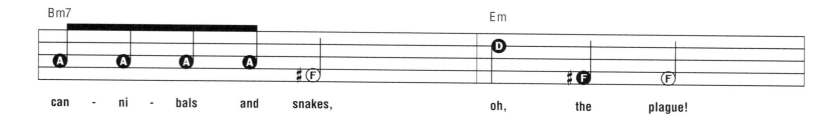

can - ni - bals and snakes, oh, the plague!

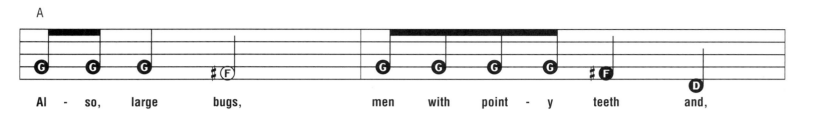

Al - so, large bugs, men with point - y teeth and,

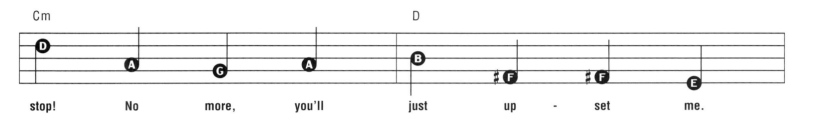

stop! No more, you'll just up - set me.

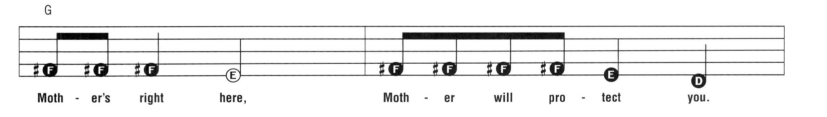

Moth - er's right here, Moth - er will pro - tect you.

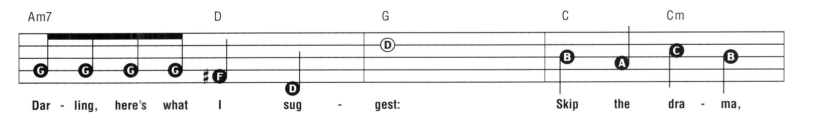

Dar - ling, here's what I sug - gest: Skip the dra - ma,

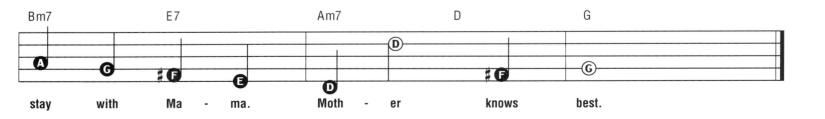

stay with Ma - ma. Moth - er knows best.

SOMETHING THAT I WANT
from Walt Disney Pictures' TANGLED

Music and Lyrics by
Grace Potter

HAPPY WORKING SONG
from Walt Disney Pictures' ENCHANTED

Music by Alan Menken
Lyrics by Stephen Schwartz

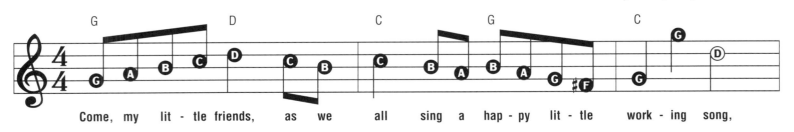

Come, my lit - tle friends, as we all sing a hap - py lit - tle work - ing song,

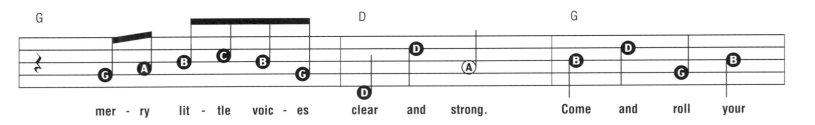

mer - ry lit - tle voic - es clear and strong. Come and roll your

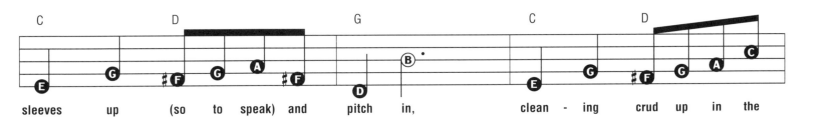

sleeves up (so to speak) and pitch in, clean - ing crud up in the

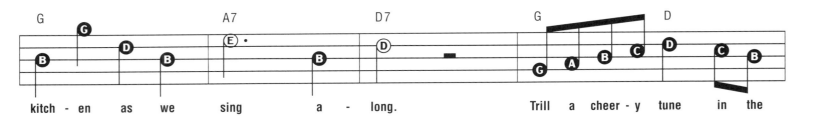

kitch - en as we sing a - long. Trill a cheer - y tune in the

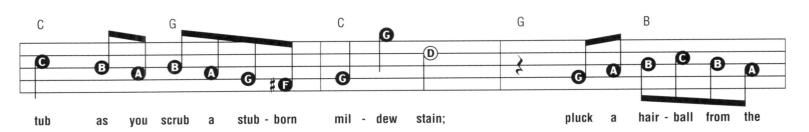

tub as you scrub a stub - born mil - dew stain; pluck a hair - ball from the

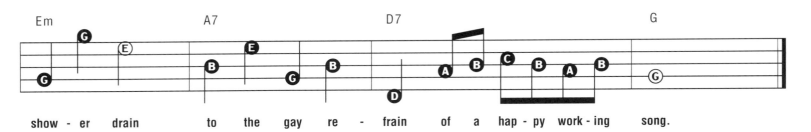

show - er drain to the gay re - frain of a hap - py work - ing song.

THAT'S HOW YOU KNOW

from Walt Disney Pictures' ENCHANTED

Music by Alan Menken
Lyrics by Stephen Schwartz

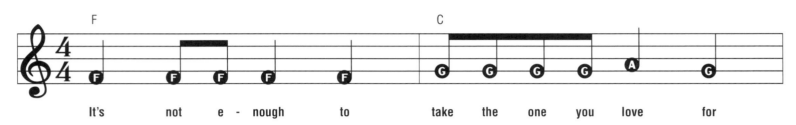

It's not e - nough to take the one you love for

grant - ed. ____ You must re - mind her,

or she'll be in - clined to say: "How do I

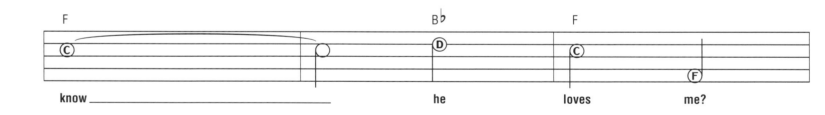

know ____ he loves me?

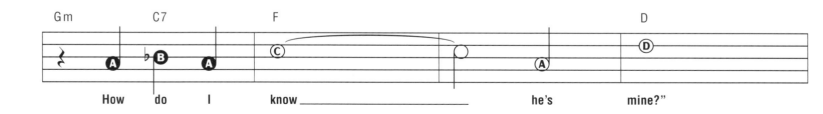

How do I know ____ he's mine?"

23

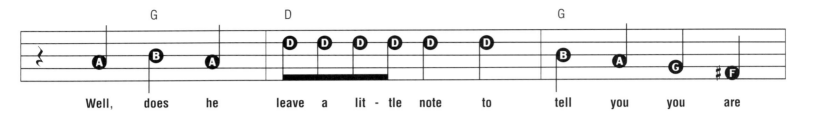

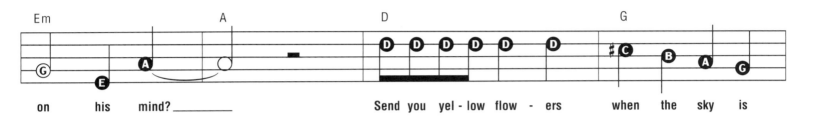

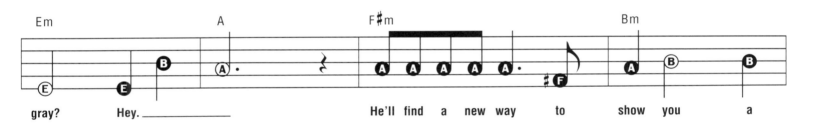

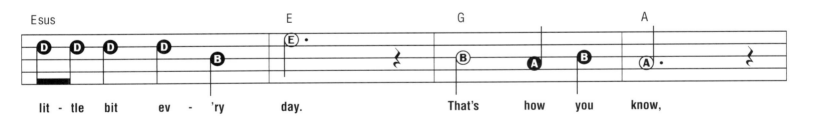

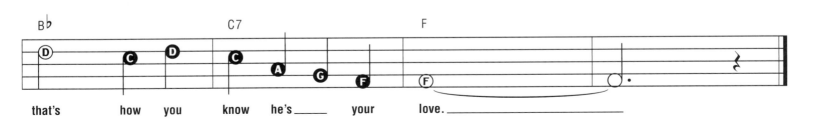

TRUE LOVE'S KISS
from Walt Disney Pictures' ENCHANTED

Music by Alan Menken
Lyrics by Stephen Schwartz

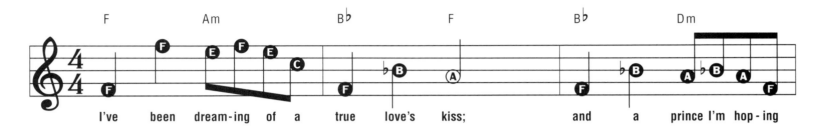

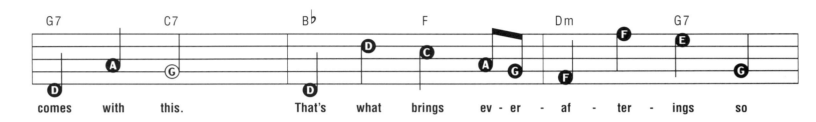

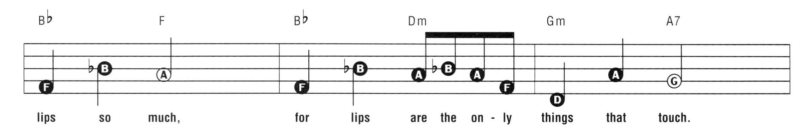

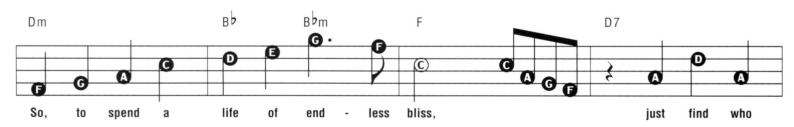

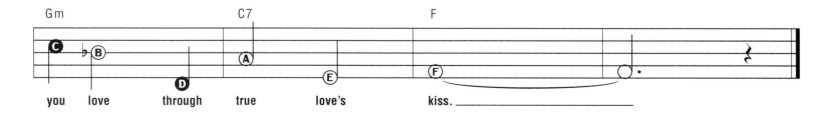